Rest

— for the rest of us

by Tim Foley

Copyright © 2020 by The Salvation Army

Published by Crest Books

Crest Books
The Salvation Army National Headquarters
615 Slaters Lane
Alexandria, VA 22313
Phone: 703-684-5523

Lt. Colonel Tim Foley, *National Secretary for Program & Editor-in-Chief*
Alexanderia Saurman, *Editorial Assistant*
Joshua Morales, *Lead Graphic Designer*
Ashley Schena, *Graphic Designer*
Elizabeth Hanley, *Electronic Communications Specialist*

Available in print from crestbooks.com

ISBN: 978-1-946709-18-9

Printed in the United States of America

All rights reserved. No part of this publication may be reproduced, stores in a retrieval system, or transmitted in any form or by any means without prior written permission of the publisher. Exceptions are brief quotations in printed reviews.

Dedication

To my wife, Cindy, who has graciously allowed and tolerated my inner child to come out often and play in this very adult world we have roamed together for over thirty-five years.

"Rest even from the thought of labor." ~ Abraham Herschel

"Sabbath dissolves the artificial urgency of our days, because it liberates us from the need to be finished." ~ Walt Mueller

"Primarily, I have lost my soul to one of the chief rivals of devotion to Christ—that is, service for Him." ~ Howard Baker

"The soil of the soul must be tended, and cultivation only comes in the slower moments of life." ~ Tim Foley

Contents

Foreword   vii

Preface   xi

1. Absence: Creating space in our lives   1

2. Commanded: Obeying in the light of grace   7

3. Slowing: Learning the art of intentional pacing   13

4. Recreating: Restoring one's self   19

5. Delight: Defining joy in our lives   27

6. Celebration: Delight in the life we have been given   35

7. Ceasing: Hitting the stop button   39

8. Sabbath: We rest to work   43

9. A Day Off: The call to something different   49

10. So What?: Further steps to take   55

Epilogue   59

Acknowledgments   61

Recommended Reading   63

About the Author   67

Foreword

By Stephen A. Macchia

God is pro work. He created the world and then he sat back and enjoyed the fruit of his labor.

He loves fruitfulness, especially when it honors him.

Therefore, we can immediately surmise: God loves those who do the most good.

The Salvation Army. The faithful, called out, gifted and set apart ones. Known by their good deeds. Blessed for their multiplying efforts in presenting the Good News of the Gospel of Jesus Christ and in serving the lost, the least, and the lonely.

God is also pro rest. He was the first to practice Sabbath. And, he invited and commanded his followers to do likewise.

He loves lingering, especially when it honors him.

Therefore, we can immediately surmise: God loves those who rest and learn how to do nothing really well.

The Salvation Army. The blessed, forgiven, commissioned and empowered. Known by their love. Blessed for their globally focused prayers for the fullness of God's Spirit and the reconciling nature of the ministry of grace and mercy and love toward all who cross their path.

So, which of the above sentiments fit your paradigm? Tim Foley hopes that both of them resonate with your heart, mind, body, and soul. Why? Because he's introducing herein a radical concept for a community of servant leaders who have been commissioned to do the most good for everyone, every day, and in every place around the globe. That profound concept: sabbath rest.

"Doing the most good" is the motto we adore. It's on every piece of stationary, every coffee cup, and every truck panel affiliated with the Salvation Army. It's more than what you do—it's who you are. Salvationists to the core and in the corps.

Learning how to "be the most rested" is the motto presented here in this timely text. Being the most rested is actually what will feed you to do the most good. Sound a bit upside down? Then you've turned to the right place; the book you are holding in your hands will be your guide.

Sabbath rest is not for the spiritually elite. It's for the rest of us too. It's not an optional extra, just for those who are committed to a life of prayer or inhabit a monastic community. No, sabbath rest is for all to embrace as part of a lifestyle of holiness and devotion to Christ.

Sabbath rest is good for your body. And your mind. And your heart. And your soul. It's all encompassing and it's a pure gift, pure gold for all who seek rest in God. For when we rest in God, we discover the rest of God, and in resting in God we find deeper, more life-changing peace in God. In rest we learn to trust and when we trust, then we bear fruit for his kingdom and glory.

It's simple and profound. It's common and unique. Especially in a world filled with distraction, noise, discord, and unrest. It's time we walk at a different pace than the rest of the world. It's time we embrace a new way of being restful in our world.

When I grew up there were "blue laws" that hindered most activity on Sunday, with the exception of going to church or the hospital. When the blue laws disappeared, nearly overnight we became a 24/7 culture. Perhaps it's time we returned to "God's law" and reinstate Sabbath as the fourth and no-longer-to-be-ignored-or-avoided Commandment. Seeing sabbath as something that reflects the heart and heartbeat of God and embracing sabbath as an invitation and gift from God, we will indeed walk to the beat of a different drummer…the heart-pounding priority of Jesus himself.

You see, with sabbath as the turnkey to the deeper life, once experienced and enjoyed, there's no turning back to the wilderness and the wildness of 24/7 living. Ceasing from our work, resting and trusting God, celebrating our life in God, and embracing the fullness of our life with God are keys to the abundant life. Once tasted, the thirst will reemerge from within the wellspring of your heart and soul. Let your taste buds come alive in sabbath living and watch how your life is changed right before your eyes—and in the hearts of all you serve.

Tim Foley is on to something BIG here. Read this text with intensity and openness, and the Spirit of God will transform your view of Sabbath—biblically, relationally, and holistically. As a result, your slowing down will lead to your becoming more. More loving. More patient. More graced. More forgiving. More holy. More fruitful for God's Kingdom.

To the God of work and rest we offer this book. May it be abundantly and richly blessed, especially in the hearts and lives of those who do the most good, the worldwide family of The Salvation Army.

With a grateful heart in Christ, the Lord of the Sabbath,

Stephen A. Macchia, M.Div., D.Min.
Founder and President, Leadership Transformations, Inc.
Director, Pierce Center for Disciple-Building
Adjunct Faculty, Gordon-Conwell Theological Seminary

Preface

Look closely at the opening shot of each episode of the American public television show *Mister Rogers' Neighborhood* and you will see the traffic light flashing yellow. A flashing yellow light alerts us to be cautious. It was a subtle signal to even the youngest viewers to slow down, that it was okay to pause and focus their attention.

Mr. Rogers would come into the house singing the now famous song, "It's a beautiful day in the neighborhood." He would take off his suit jacket, replace it with a cardigan, take off his dress shoes, and put on sneakers. That was one of the most mesmerizing and memorable entrances ever into a television show. Just mentioning these items, those familiar with the show can recall it in the mind's eye and hear it with the inner ear. He would intentionally talk slowly and clearly and pause deliberately. Great things would occur in each episode and viewers could absorb them thanks to the show's intentional slow cadence.

Where do you find the television shows today that tell you to slow down? Who is speaking up to say, "Take it easy, pace yourself"? We are accustomed to a fast-paced life. We have come to expect instant results. We demand a myriad of choices when it comes to food, clothes, and other consumable goods. Taking time to slow down is for some simply a waste of time. We want to go faster, quicker. We have no time for the slow lane. Our flitting attention spans resemble that of a gnat. We have a hard time focusing. We run. We scoot. We hurry. Slow down? Forget it.

What happens when we do finally allow ourselves to take the time and slow down some?

We discover something so simple it's almost magical and overwhelming: we find we have created more space in our lives to think and to do. We begin to discover. We fall in love with the idea of wonder. We begin to tap into our imaginations. We begin to see visions. We find inspiration again.

What you are about to read in the following pages is an attempt to draw your attention to that change of pace you may desperately need. Slowing has a natural appeal and a curiosity to us, yet it's allusive and can be quite difficult to conqueror so you can rediscover that spark of inspiration and wonder within.

Many moons ago, I was interviewed for my application to gain entry into The Salvation Army's training college. The Divisional Commander gave me only one bit of advice: "Tim, always beware of the machinery." At the time I had no clue what this riddle meant, but over the course of my journey in ministry, I came to fully understand this statement. Machines have no soul. They have a single purpose: to produce. The machinery of ministry (or any type of work) will eat the average person alive if there is no attention paid to the need for rest and recreation.

The topic of sabbath is one that is trending in all of Christendom these days. No matter one's generation, theological persuasion, geographical location, ethnicity, gender, or age, this topic is more timely than ever. The issue of sabbath strikes a nerve and activates the vocal cords of many. This matter can easily trigger passionate responses that can be enlightening, engaging, and troubling at the same time.

The mass of information available on the topic of the sabbath, with the simple push of a button or the turn of the page, is vast and somewhat overwhelming. This can add to the confusion and the perplexity of the subject.

So why another book about it?

In 2012, I started pursuing a doctorate in Spiritual Formation for Ministry Leaders from Gordon Conwell Theological Seminary in South Hamilton, Massachusetts. In coming up with a thesis challenge for my dissertation, the term "sabbath" immediately came to mind in connection with spiritual formation and my own ministry experience within The Salvation Army.

This topic is not something that has been written on or even spoken about extensively within the context of my denomination.

"We will work till Jesus comes" is a favorite lyric and philosophy of the spirit-filled and totally engaged Salvationist. As inspiring as this can be, it is in all reality the crux of the problem. It's quite difficult for a passionate, driven, and divinely called social activist to slow down. There is a world in pain, bleeding from festering emotional, mental, and spiritual wounds. The call to "rescue the perishing" still rings forth. There is no stopping in this fight for good. Keep going. Keep grinding. Never stop.

But the simple reality is this: if there is no time for rest and reflection, then the whole process begins to become unbalanced and unwinds rapidly into a negative spiral. If there is no intentionality in the teaching on the matter of the sabbath, then it doesn't enter into the mindset and culture of the individual nor into the culture of The Salvation Army or whatever ministry or work is involved.

I have seen people crash with my own eyes. I have witnessed marriages that fell apart and lives forever shattered. Covenants forgotten and pushed aside. A divine call once so crystal clear silenced and ignored. Much of this could have been avoided by simply taking time to keep things in check, the soul balanced, and the physical body maintained.

Over the course of a year, I explored the issue of sabbath with the active officer force of The Salvation Army Western Territory. I surveyed 750 active officers in this particular region of the United States. I gave a window of three weeks to respond and only sent out one reminder. I had set an optimistic goal of getting 150 responses back, which would have been well above the norms for a doctoral research project. Within the first twenty-four hours, I had over 200 responses. In total, 590 individuals responded to the survey overall. I realized at that moment I had touched a raw nerve.

The purpose of the project was to determine if the topic of sabbath rest is in the heart and mind of an active Salvation Army officer. Is there a clear definition of sabbath? What sorts of challenges lie in the way in making sabbath a habit in the life of an officer? Are there institutional challenges that get in the way from preventing an officer to embrace sabbath?

The results were published in May 2015 in the thesis project now on file in the library of Gordon Conwell Theological Seminary. The responses varied. The overall consensus of those who participated in the survey is that they do not practice sabbath for numerous reasons.

Mainly, it comes down to one thing in general: the duties of the ministry get in the way. The ever-hounding echoes of the tyranny of the urgent persist. The to-do lists are overflowing. The work never ceases. The burden keeps growing. Scope creep settles in. The expectations are endless. Managing all of this becomes muddled, murky, and suffocating.

This book is not to highlight the "faults" of those who are not in a regular habit of taking sabbath. There is no finger pointing or casting judgment here. This book is not a comprehensive theological summation of the entire topic of sabbath rest. This book is not to blame anyone. I am not interested in arguing the differing views of how sabbath is interpreted. Arguing theology bores me and really serves zero purpose.

This exercise of writing, thinking, reflecting, and challenging only works if I can get one individual to a place where he or she can acknowledge the need for balance in their life, then actually do something about it.

Much of what I have studied and focus on here is of critical importance for anyone considering engaging in a life of active ministry, regardless of the denomination. What follows also applies to anyone who realizes that their life is out of balance and needs to be recalibrated.

This topic is not to promote self-care over sacrifice. The role of the person involved in full-time service requires dedication, commitment, living the surrendered life, and self-sacrifice. The reality is that we in The Salvation Army do not keep bankers' hours, nor are we promised a day off. We are encouraged to use our brains and to learn how to listen to our bodies. We have a natural alert system that reminds us that we cannot keep a constant on the go pace. Certainly, that would be total nonsense and breaking one of God's commands when it comes to rest.

I will give some clarity, in a brief narrative format, of what sabbath is and is not and how we must push this to the forefront of our thinking. Finding the balance is the key, but always a tricky task in this journey of faith.

May you find in the pages that follow inspiration to enter the joy of rest God created for us.

Tim Foley, Lt. Colonel
National Secretary for Program & Editor in Chief
The Salvation Army National Headquarters
Alexandria, Virginia. Summer 2020

Chapter ONE

~ *Absence* ~
Creating space in our lives

"I was trying to daydream, but my mind kept wandering."
~ Steven Wright

Daydreaming has long been both a problem and a benefit to me. I can often get lost wandering in my mind, escaping the challenges in front of me on my real-life path. Yet, I do find perspective once I start daydreaming of my past. In moments of difficulty, I often find myself reflecting on my childhood memories. Those memories tend to calm me and assure me that things are going to be okay.

I was fortunate to grow up in a rural part of America, the Napa Valley of California. Frequently, my buddies and I would run around the prune orchards that thrived in the fields across the street from my home. We would make tree forts in the autumn that would become our hideaways in winter. In the spring we would run through the fields full of tall mustard weeds swaying in the breeze. We would crawl around on the ground like squirrels, tunneling our way through the grass. The summertime would bring out the ripe fruit which we would pick to either eat or throw at each other. We mostly threw them. Reality check: one can only eat so many fresh prunes in a day.

Life was just different back then. We played nearly all day long, from the early sunlight until the streetlights came on. We rode our bikes. Fished in the local creeks. Flew our kites in the strong spring winds. Made our own baseball field in an empty lot. We swam in an above the ground pool that my dad put up in our backyard until the wrinkles on our skin appeared to be permanent. We dug holes in the backyard hoping for a passage to China. We burned our trash and set fire to the fallen leaf piles in the autumn. I know some might find that ecologically ignorant, but it was a simpler time.

Rare was heard the phrase: "I am bored." We just did stuff. We didn't have computers or game consoles. If we were fortunate, we had a transistor radio. The television had four channels to choose from and would sign off the air at midnight. We slept. We ate. We laughed. We cried. We fell down. We got back up again. We used our imaginations. We took flight in our dreams.

Then things changed. We grew up. Seemingly overnight our lives were flooded with decisions to be made and choices to be wrestled with. We moved from our innocent childhoods into the pain of the real world. We began to ask the questions. "Why was the President killed?" "What again is the reason for this war we are in?" "What's in a body bag?" "What exactly is a 'Watergate?'"

We became aware of the world around us and began to immerse ourselves in all of its trappings. We were guided to follow preprogrammed steps: "Here is the path. Walk in it." College. Career. Companion. Matrimony. Children. Responsibilities. Ownership. A host of other challenges. The list grew long and high of the path we needed to take.

Suddenly, we had no time for anything. Then technology came sweeping in with its broad promise to make our lives easier.

We now pay for apps on our phones that are supposed to make us calm and allow us to produce more in each of our days. We believed the exaggeration that technology promised simplicity in our life and at times are worse for the wear for it. We have become addicted to our devices. We habitually look at the blue screen rather than into the eyes of our neighbors. It has affected everything from our sleep patterns to our personal relationships.

Absence

We are now instantly accessible to the world. Technology has become the new idol of our times.

What we have lost in the process of all of this is permission to give ourselves space. To give ourselves permission to just do nothing. To discover that it's okay to be bored and let our minds wander. To learn that daydreaming, pondering, and pausing is part of the natural order to things. Putting up the "do not disturb" placard on our doors from time to time is truly a great thing.

To do nothing is considered a waste of time for some but not from God's perspective. Learning to live with absence takes both discipline and initiative. Creating space allows us to be mindful of others and attentive to the situations of life that surround us. It beckons, regardless of our temperament or the thought that sitting in silence isn't for me.

One of my unique experiences in high school was in an English class in which the teacher constantly challenged us to broaden our horizons when it came to honing our critical thinking skills. She would remind us over and over that we needed to learn to think for ourselves and not believe everything we hear or read.

She was particularly concerned about us teens becoming addicted to television. As a teen of that era, I can confess I had a strong tendency to do so. One of her favorite quotes was from the sociologist Marshall McLuhan, who rightly predicted the influence of media when he said, "The medium is the message." The nature of a medium, or channel used to share a message, is more important than the content of the message that is given. It was in that class I learned how to give myself space from what the TV was throwing out and how to process the messages into appropriate meanings. Turn the TV off. Turn the volume down to zero. Step outside. Take in the fresh air and the beautiful sights all around. See the ants do their work of preparation for the coming winter. Listen to the bird's chime and sing to each other. Look at the people moving about. In other words, I learned early in my life to be aware of my surroundings and to become more self-aware. I learned to understand my limitations and to accept them.

When Jerusalem was under siege, the prophet Jeremiah was

given the unenviable job of speaking words of truth to a population that was in no mood to listen. Jeremiah reminded the people to stop and pause: This is what the Lord says: "Stop at the crossroads and look around. Ask for the old, Godly way, and walk in it. Travel its path, and you will find rest for your souls. But you reply, 'No, that's not the road we want!'"[1]

There is an ancient path that has been long marked as the best way for us to go. God set it up for all of us to safely journey on. Sadly, we continue to deviate from it. We get easily distracted. We see things that catch our attention elsewhere. A shiny ribbon dangling on a branch just off the path draws us away. It could be the latest gadget or thinking there must be a better way.

Jeremiah's words speak to us today. Our lives are under siege by so many messages and distractions. It's not easy to just stop. The Hebrew word here not only means to stand still in one place but also to stop and take a stand. It means to stand firm. With that sense of standing comes the idea of being persistent in how we remain true to what we believe and enduring the onslaught about to come our way.

We don't need to keep pushing ourselves to find some place of personal prestige that quickly passes away or obtain material possessions that pile up, eventually becoming debris. Moving about in a real cadence in our lives allows us to habitually stop and rest which allows us the time and energy to shore up what really matters in our lives.

When we are overwhelmed, we know that this is what we must do. We must stop. But often we ignore this. When I am driving to someplace new and using my GPS to find it, I still can get lost. Rather than pulling my car over and stopping to actually ask someone for directions, I try to outsmart my GPS and others by attempting to figure out a better way on my own, only to find that I waste more time, frustrate myself, and get lost in the process.

Creating space in our lives doesn't happen automatically. We can't download a fancy app on our phones for this, though some would attempt to convince us to do so. We can't seek the advice from others to do it for us. We must do it ourselves. Carving out time to stop, assess, and reorient ourselves is up to us. There is an element of self-control and discipline that we must take on.

We may need to drop some of the things in our lives that crowds the daily schedule or adds to the sense of confusion. Allowing for absence, or intentionally reducing stuff that we truly may not need or can live without for the time being, may in the long run be so beneficial to us we can't even begin to comprehend the full value.

Where is the good way? Ask. Ask people to keep you accountable. Take inventory of how you use your time. We each have 168 hours a week to spend. What are we doing with those moments and minutes?

Then when you either see or sense it, walk in it. In other words, just do it. Cut this out. Stop doing that. Quit blaming the company you work for or the church in which you serve in. You still take a paycheck? You still have to work. Don't shortchange the company or denomination you work for. Knock off the excuse making. Own up to the fact that your life is packed with things you just need to stop doing. Fill your schedule up with space to breathe and think and dream.

Let go of the excuses which only lead to stubborn rebellion and eventual destruction, and that caused the crowd in Jeremiah's day to say: "We will not walk in it."

There will always be distractions and interruptions. Life happens. Change comes. Surprises emerge that we weren't expecting. But you can simply stay the course when you allow absence of doing in your life to be more of the common experience than the rare occasion.

The choice is really up to you to make it happen. So, go build a fort or dig a hole to China. It will do your soul a world of good.

Questions for reflection
What is stopping you from just standing still?

What is holding you back from finding true rest in your soul?

Take inventory of the 168 hours in the week allotted to you. Where are you creating time to breathe and think and dream?

Chapter TWO

~ *Commanded* ~
Obeying in the light of grace

"If you can't take a nap, if you can't take a day off, heaven's going to drive you nuts."
~ Mark Driscoll

I have always been a rule abider. There are many in this world who like to go outside the lines on purpose, who like to push the standards, dangle on the edge, and question everything. Me? I like to abide. I am more comfortable staying within the lines where the path is known and safe.

I remember the incredibly guilty feeling that came over my mind on "senior cut day" at my high school. A long-standing tradition allowed seniors to "legally" skip a day in the few couple of weeks before the end of the academic year. Throughout my elementary and secondary education, I always made it a point to be in class. In a few instances, I missed a school day because of illness, but overall my attendance record was impeccable.

It's a simple rule: when school is in session, you attend class. Period. So, when my friends invited me to join them to spend the day at a local lake, I felt miserable the whole time. I felt like I was really doing something wrong. I didn't feel right until I got home from that "illegal" activity. Looking back, my response to all of that was sort of silly. But it spoke to the type of person I was, really still am in many ways.

In my ministry path over the decades, God has had a unique

way of placing me in situations that forced me to expand the boundaries. Maintaining the status quo may work in some particular settings, but it never seemed par for the course for me. Methods have to change over the course of time, but the mission focus shouldn't ever change or be diverted. It sounds great and wonderful to talk about developing new methodology, but how do I deal with that when I am comfortable with methods as they are? Staying in the lines is safe. Next thing I know, God wants me to expand my boundaries. Really tough to do.

The Ten Commandments that God gave to the Hebrews in their exodus from Egypt had both form and function.[2] These former slaves needed lines. God provided the safe zone. Solid boundaries were set in place. "This is off limits. Do this instead." They needed a strong sense of guidance. The first of these four commandments dealt with individual obedience. The remaining six dispensed with life and how it was to be lived with others in the community. In all reality, the commandments really offer sound advice for an individual who wants to thrive in his or her lifetime.

The first command was a strong reminder that the God they were following was the only God they would ever need. Coming out of a land that celebrated many different gods caused confusion and a natural tendency for a person to wander away. The one true God was not going to be just one of the many gods to be added to the Egyptians long list of deities. The first three commands deal with misunderstanding who God is; making sure they remained focused on only serving one God and stopping them from misusing his name with vows they never intended to keep.

Then comes the Sabbath. The fourth commandment deals with one day in their week to set aside for worship and rest.

"Remember to observe the Sabbath day by keeping it holy."[3]

Think of it as God holding up a big stop sign in his hand. We seriously need to come to a complete stop. With this command, God knew what he was doing. He reminded the Hebrews that they were still human beings despite all of the great things they had accomplished in their lives. God knew even greater things were still to come for them, if they intentionally maintained balance between work and rest.

With this commandment comes a distinct need for trust. While roaming around the desert, God took care of his people by providing for them. There were no "big box stores" for the nearly three million people to shop at. What they had to eat came from above. The provision of manna, a bread like substance, and the quail that fell from the sky that filled their daily protein intake were indeed a daily miracle. Every day, the people would go out and collect what they needed for that day only. But on the sixth day of the week, God provided a double portion of what they would need to cover them for the Sabbath.[4]

Most of the people prepared for their rest day. Of course, some never did and ended up with empty stomachs on the Sabbath. They failed to collect the double portion and did not trust to take God at his word.

The fourth commandment is loaded with significance: if we don't rest, we will fall apart. Our bodies were never designed without the thought of slowing down to rest. When we don't rest, there is a natural progression that begins to settle in rather quickly. Creative energy departs. Mental fatigue sets in. Physical ailments begin to beset us. Stress settles in to suppress and depress us to the point where we can no longer think clearly. All the way around, the lack of rest is no good for us.

If we are not careful, we can easily replace God in our lives by making work our personal idol. Ambition takes over and we become driven. We manage our lives by optics: how does this look to others? Will I be viewed as a "slacker" if I check my pace and even stop? I must do, do, and do again. Until Jesus comes. Stop? Not hardly.

This is a triple challenge for anyone involved in "activist" type ministry where "need knows no season." Caring for others, saving the planet, and ending all pain and suffering is a 24/7 job, right? Wrong. The command still applies even to the most warrior minded of us. Even Jesus reminded us, tenderly, that the poor will always be with us.[5] Life with all its pain and suffering doesn't stop. But that doesn't exclude us from doing so periodically.

Pausing for sabbath rest helps all of this to be reset in our lives. Direction. Focus. Jesus simply reminds us, "The Sabbath was made for man, not man for the Sabbath. So, the Son of Man is Lord even of the Sabbath."[6] We rest to work.

Things got out of hand quickly with Sabbath laws by the time it got into the minds of the Pharisees. We find in Mark's gospel two instances where the Pharisees went out of their way to condemn the "work" of Jesus, when he performed healing on the Sabbath day.[7] Jesus walked through a field with his disciples on the Sabbath and some of them picked some dangling strands of wheat. It nearly cost them their lives. One Sabbath day as Jesus was walking through some grain fields, his disciples began breaking off heads of grain to eat. But the Pharisees said to Jesus, "Look, why are they breaking the law by harvesting grain on the Sabbath?" Jesus said to them, "Haven't you ever read in the Scriptures what David did when he and his companions were hungry? He went into the house of God (during the days when Abiathar was high priest) and broke the law by eating the sacred loaves of bread that only the priests are allowed to eat. He also gave some to his companions." Then Jesus said to them, "The Sabbath was made to meet the needs of people, and not people to meet the requirements of the Sabbath.[8]

The claim of them working on the Sabbath resounded forth from the Pharisees. How did things get like this? Since when did the legal beagles need to invade the lives of individuals in such a manner?

Jesus challenged the Pharisees by using a scripture account they knew well. Jesus points to David when he ate "the consecrated bread" as something that the priests of the temple habitually did.[9] When God was present to the Israelites in the temple he had them build, there were twelve loaves of bread, known as the "Bread of the Presence," that were placed on the holy table in the temple each Sabbath. The priests were able to eat the leftovers when the bread was exchanged out for the new loaves.

Jesus was calling on the Pharisees to use some common sense and to remember what the priests were allowed to do. Over time, the Pharisees fell in love with an obsession over every finite detail regarding how each of the commandments were to be played out in ordinary life. The Sabbath was no exception.

In all truth, what happened to them is what happens to us. We set a law in place which in many instances is to be a guideline to assist us as individuals and maintain safety for life in the community. A policy is set in place that seemingly is there to protect the common order of things. Then some people choose not to obey or abide by said laws. That's when it all gets dicey.

For instance, common sense would dictate that it's pretty dumb to text and drive while using hand-held devices. Yet, people are killed every year because of that action. Distracted driving now rises to the top of illegal activity on the road and needs to be governed by strict laws. In many places, a violation comes with stiff penalties and fines. All because some people fail to use their brains and succumb to FOMO,[10] or the fear of missing out on the moment.

Over the centuries, the Pharisees took all of the commandments and kept expanding their interpretation. They set into place rules of conduct that became overkill. The purpose of the law was lost. The original intent of what God had in mind for his people became muddled. The version of what the commandment meant was stretched to some unbelievable and unattainable measures.

In short, the Sabbath laws became more important than the original purpose of the Sabbath itself. The obsession of making rules and making sure everyone abided by them took over. What was lost in all of this was the fact that God created the Sabbath as a day of delight for his creation. It had become a day of burden. It was no longer enjoyable and turned somewhat into a day of dread.

Sabbath has nothing to do with a particular day of the week. In this day and age, people have to work on Sundays. Many people have to work two, if not three, jobs to keep a roof over their heads and food on the table for their families. I work in a profession that technically is on the clock 24/7. Our society is built on the expectation that things will run at full capacity at all times. Taking an entire day off is nearly impossible for many. Does that mean we are doomed? Under the old laws, yes. Well, at least according to the men who interpreted them as such. But under the realm of grace we can seek to find ways to experience the day of delight. Maybe taking a whole twenty-four hours off a week isn't possible for you. But what about breaking that up into time segments that will work? Space that time off over the work week. Learn to listen to your body. Give yourself permission to stop. Find a way that works for you in this particular season of your life.

Commands have a place and purpose in our lives today. They are not meant to act as a noose around our necks to hang us by. They are not archaic and relative to another era. In essence, they can act as guidelines that allow us to engage in our world with more grace and civility. Consider what God says to remind us to rest. Taking deliberate time to relish in our day of delight will allow us to thrive and abide in the life God intended.

Questions for reflection
How do you measure up in regard to keeping the command of sabbath rest?

What would make Sabbath truly a day of delight for you?

What is your view about living a life with all work and no play?

Chapter THREE

~ *Slowing* ~
Learning the art of intentional pacing

"I spent a lifetime in a garden one afternoon."
~ Craig D. Lounsbrough

The street I live on has "speed humps." In case you don't know what that is, just simply replace the "h" with a "b" in the "umps." Figure it out? You don't normally see a residential street with speed bumps, but we were the extremely lucky ones to have one. [Insert frazzled look here.]

This particular street cuts through fairways from a main highway to the local high school. At certain parts of the day, the traffic volume and the speed of the cars traversing the road increases rapidly. The majority of the cars at the high peak travel time are driven by teenage drivers, meaning the street quickly fills up with inexperienced, fast, young drivers at the busiest hours.

Backing out of our driveway can be challenging. Looking both ways is normal but looking to the left is more of a challenge because our view of oncoming traffic is blocked by cars parked on the street. What makes it worse is that there is a slight hill the cars come over which obscures their view.

For the most part, drivers obey the speed limit. We haven't experienced any accidents. A local police officer patrols the area on occasion to watch the traffic for a while and then moves on.

My wife and I have had to establish two important habits when it comes to navigating out of our driveway and into the street. The first rule is never be in a hurry. Nothing good can come from backing out of our driveway too fast. The other rule is leave before the morning rush. The pacing on the street becomes hurried between 7:50 and 8:05 a.m., simply because school starts at 8:15. This is what I call intentional pacing in our commute. We must move slowly because we have to. It's the smart thing to do. Now, it's an ingrained habit. Some habits of learning to go slow come about naturally. We must go slow as we back out, otherwise it would become an expensive disaster as we could plow into cars on a constant basis. We must pay attention to the clock as to when it's best to get moving.

Sometimes we have to adjust our pace because of a besetting physical aliment. A nagging injury to my leg may prevent me from entering a race or plodding on the treadmill like I am used to. That's only natural; persistent pain sounds the alarm for us to stop. Other cues cause us to adjust our pace. We may feel the tug on our arm from a small hand that says, "Mama, will you have time to play with me after work?" The boss who reminds us to monitor our time better, since key details on a project are being overlooked, also signals a need for change.

But how do we slow ourselves when there is no painful alarm going off to warn us that we can't keep going at this pace? When we have no hand tugging ours? No sound of the boss' voice is heard. How do we just learn to slowly press on the brakes of life?

In a classic passage of scripture, often recited during a wedding ceremony, the Apostle Paul reminds us of some lasting truth.[11] In the first three verses, he uses metaphors that emphasize mystery, loftiness, individual greatness, speaking in tongues, the ability to predicate amazing things of the future, or being filled with every kind of knowledge possible. He hits on self-proclaiming saintly behavior: giving of all I have to the poor and enduring every amount of suffering.

When the Apostle Paul's words are recited during a wedding ceremony in the beauty of the chapel, with the stunning bride, the handsome groom, and all the décor of the perfect wedding, he lets the hammer fly with the words echoing off the walls: "But if I have not love, I gain nothing."[12]

Truth. We are nothing. Nada. Zip. Talk about a downer. He gives a step ladder to love in succeeding verses by sharing what it is and isn't.

"Love is patient and kind. Love is not jealous or boastful or proud or rude. It does not demand its own way. It is not irritable, and it keeps no record of being wronged. It does not rejoice about injustice but rejoices whenever the truth wins out. Love never gives up, never loses faith, is always hopeful, and endures through every circumstance."[13]

I am sure he could have kept on going to add to this growing list of dos and don'ts when it comes to loving others.

The first word catches my attention: patience. The idea here is that love is something that is unhurried. It takes time to develop in relationships. Paul seems to be sending us a strong reminder here that it's not always all about us, our needs, what we want, or where to go to get it.

A story is told of a monk who had little if any patience with himself or anyone. The more he tried to be patient, the more impatient he became. He came up with a plan to improve his patience. He decided to get away from everything and everybody. He found himself a little piece of land buried deep in the woods and built for himself a little home where he would live in isolation.

Many years later, a man traveling through the woods came across the monk in his home. The man was quite shocked to find the monk living out in the middle of nowhere, away from the rest of the world.

"Why are you living out here in these far-removed woods all by yourself?" the man inquired.

"I am here to learn how to be patient." the monk replied.

The man was curious. "How long have you lived here?"

"Seven years."

The man didn't know how quite to respond but quickly thought of something: "If there is no one around you to bother you, how will you know when you are patient?"

Taking a moment to think about it, the annoyed monk replied, "Get away from me, I have no time for you."

To be patient means to learn to endure. In a relationship where there is no equal giving and sharing, things quickly get out of balance. Adjustments need to be made. Just as we back slowly out of the driveway into a busy street, so must we un-hurry ourselves in relationship building. Things take time to develop. A relationship needs room to roam and blossom. It not only needs space but also time. Unhurried time. We must work with each other and avoid transferring our sense of perfection on others.

In the course of my years in ministry, I have conducted more funerals than marriages. But one of the marriage ceremonies we participated in stands out above the rest. It wasn't about the actual ceremony in the church. It was the news that came to me about a month later, after all the wedding hoopla had faded away.

The couple informed me that they were simply going to have their marriage annulled due to the fact that they could not agree on how to handle their joint finances. They found themselves arguing soon after the honeymoon dust settled on whose money was going to pay for what. Instead of taking a rational approach and setting out to figure a way to make it all work, they decided to forgo the patience love requires and call it quits. All over the mighty dollar. To this day that memory makes me sadly shake my head and think, "Why?"

Too often we are in a hurry with God. Instead of sitting and enjoying the presence of God in a slow and quiet way, we learn how to fulfill our spiritual obligations with a "gab and go" conversation with him. We may have a daily verse pop up on our phone or find ourselves liking someone's spiritual meme on Instagram instead of settling in for substance in our relationship with God.

The development of that love relationship takes time. It is an art form to learn to navigate these relationship waters with God. At times, there are no simple or easy formulas to follow. We may need to rely on our intuition or feelings on how to go about this.

The key is to start with your own desire and initiative. The couple that bailed out of their marriage early could have patiently found a path to success by taking time to think through workable alternatives. Not agreeing to financial matters was an excuse to cop out of a relationship that was on shaky ground to begin with. Recalibrating your daily pace may need to occur to find that balance you need in all of your relationships. Something has got to give to maintain a sense of balance.

Many years ago, I ran across an old Japanese proverb that said, "Never be afraid of moving slowly. Be afraid of not moving." I have used that as my personal mantra ever since, especially when I am about to embark on something that is a huge challenge and will greatly disrupt my life as I know it.

Try to start by not being in a hurry when it comes to the time you need to center yourself in God's presence. Find space in your living arrangements or outdoors to set apart as the place for you to meet. I habitually have my alone time with God each morning, usually with a cup of coffee in one hand, my bible on my lap (or iPad with a Bible app), and my hand scratching the nose of our dog, Maggie. It's by far the most enjoyable part of my day. This habit has been long in the making as much as my schedule permits, I start the slow ascent of most of my days in this fashion. I only wished I started this earlier in my life.

Don't be too hard on yourself if things don't come together quickly in these new patterns you want to develop. The key is to think, "I need to slow down here." Focus on intentional ways to pause. Embrace periods for reflection and processes as you move into deeper waters with God.

The soil of the soul must be tended, and cultivation only comes in the slower moments of life.

Questions for reflection

Have you developed the habit of meeting alone with God each day?

What steps do you need to take to slow down in your life?

Make a simple action plan that includes time alone with God to read his word and listen to his voice.

Learn to embrace patience in all your relationships.

Chapter FOUR

~ *Recreating* ~
Restoring one's self

"Life must be lived as play." ~ Plato

I have a confession to make. Actually, I have several confessions to make, but I am going to exercise some self-restraint here and just mention one. I do not like table games. Strike that. I despise table games. There go the party invitations. Oh well. Why? Boredom. For one. Too much competition for another. And the biggest factor: too many new details to learn. My overloaded, worn out brain just can't retain much anymore. My IQ levels are dropping. My muscle memory is almost nonexistent these days.

Going way back, I loved them. Who didn't like the board game "Candyland" as a child? The actual game board is dreamy. Vats of melted chocolate dot the artwork. Lollipops line the colorful path. Gumdrops await imaginary consumption by the would-be player. It's a bit of heaven to look at when you are a six-year-old who doesn't have a worry about sugar intake.

As we get older, we move on to more challenging games as our cognitive skills improve. Checkers. Chess. Yahtzee. Risk. And my road to ruin. Scrabble.

Let me back up here a bit. Scrabble is where my downfall began in my dislike of table games. I blame my mother-in-law for it. Please don't get me wrong. I loved my mother-in-law. I had a long, ongoing joke with her. When she would be visiting us on a Sunday, I would introduce her from the pulpit to the congregation by saying, "Happiness is seeing your mother-in-law's face on the back of a milk carton." People would twist in their seats. "How dare he!" She would smile and lightly laugh. She was always in on the joke.

Evelyn was a joy and delight. I miss her so.

I remember the time I had to say my final goodbye to her while she lay dying in her hospital bed in Portland, Oregon. We were called to be with her as her health took a turn for the worse. The doctor told her straight out in the company of family members that she was dying and that she didn't have long to live.

Silence.

"Are you sure?" she inquired.

"Positive."

I had to catch a plane back to San Diego to be with our children. My wife stayed with Evelyn, along with her siblings. Her final two weeks on earth were quite painful for her and for her family as they watched her body slowly shut down.

I have many happy memories of Evelyn spending time with us, spoiling her grandkids, and laughing at all my cornball jokes and antics. I felt like she was my biggest fan.

When Evelyn was devoting time with us, eventually she would call for the board game. Out came Scrabble on her command. She instantly turned into another person once the letters were dispensed and arranged in the wooden holders. It was game time. Focus. Determination. Domination. You could see it in her eyes.

It scared me. I knew what was coming.

She would pile the points up and my self-esteem would shrink to levels deeper than the deepest ocean. Word after word, she showed me who was boss. Back then, I liked to think I knew my words. But when you are constantly dealt the hand of x, q, y, n, and r, how could I stand a chance against my brainiac mother-in-law?

She always won.

Always.

Recreating

The mercy rule was never extended to me. And I thought I was her favorite son-in-law?

After she won, the game board was put away for safe keeping until another act of war on my intelligence was called for. She returned to the sweet Evelyn that I loved so dearly.

Even though I realized that I am not good at board games nor find my delight in them, I will occasionally submit to groupthink and play along, pretending to be fully engaged. At least for five minutes. Then. Nothing.

Eyes roam. Mind wanders. Sneak a peek at my phone. Did the General call yet? Yawns stifled. Watch viewing in full gear. Tap. Tap. Tap.

Play is vital for our well-being. It's part of the restorative process. Recreate. "Re-create." Re-make. Re-set. Final outcome: renewed.

Play can take on all shapes and forms these days, everything from playing the license plate alphabet game with the kids to using electronic game consoles. Engagement in something that is recreational really can be life transforming. The options for play are so vast it's hard to make a comprehensive list.

You can insert your favorite means of play here. A look inside of my play list reveals a few things: fiddling with my model trains or conquering the globe as a gamer playing in the virtual world of tanks.

The following is a true story from a conversation I had on a headset while playing a video game.

Voice: "How old are you mister?"
Me: "Sixty. Plus."
Long pause on the other end the headset. "Oh. Wow."
Me: "Yeah."
Voice: "No wonder you are a lame gamer."
Me: Silence.
The sound of crickets rises in the background.

I find myself becoming more open and attentive to nature around me, even right in my backyard. I enjoy playing with our lovely golden retriever, Maggie, who is aging quickly. I just like being in her presence as she lifts my soul with her wagging tail and happy disposition. She grabs a ball or stuffed toy and wiggles and moans with delight to greet me or anyone she sees. My wife and I have developed the fine art of bird watching. We love hummingbirds in particular. We follow their migration to our area. We give them names. We get excited when it's time to load up the feeders and sad when we notice their sudden, silent departure. We long for their return. Bird watching as play. It's an old age thing. Relax.

Defining play is an individual feature. It's really up to you to think about things that restore and rejuvenate you. There are a zillion things you can do that are cost effective or even free. The only cost for you is your time.

"Ah," I hear you say. "I knew there was a catch."

In Thornton Wilder's classic play, "Our Town," there is a wonderful moving scene near the closing of the third act. One of the main characters, Emily, has died from complications she experienced in childbirth.

She is transported to the graveyard on the hill that overlooks the sleepy, little New Hampshire town of Grover's Corner. Emily sits and watches her family go through the routines of their lives. She notices that, while the people are busily moving about, they are disconnected from each other. It troubles her greatly. She stands and moves into the kitchen of her childhood home. With tremendous passion, she speaks to her mother who can't see or hear her: "Oh, Mama, look at me one minute as though you really saw me. Mama, fourteen years have gone by. I'm dead. You're a grandmother, Mama! Wally's dead, too. His appendix burst on a camping trip to North Conway. We felt just terrible about it, don't you remember? But, just for a moment now we're all together. Mama, just for a moment we're happy. Let's really look at one another! I can't. I can't go on. It goes so fast. We don't have time to look at one another. I didn't realize. So, all that was going on and we never noticed. Take me back—up the hill—to my grave. But first: Wait! One more look. Good-bye, Good-bye world. Good-bye, Grover's Corners. Mama and Papa. Good-bye to clocks ticking and Mama's sunflowers. And food and coffee. And new ironed dresses and hot baths and sleeping and waking

Recreating 23

up. Oh, earth, you are too wonderful for anybody to realize you."

She speaks to the Stage Manager, who acts as the narrator throughout the entire play.

"Do any human beings ever realize life while they live it, every, every minute?"

"No. The saints and poets, maybe they do some."[14]

Sometimes we can become so pretentious in our daily living that we are not even self-aware. We get so caught up in what we must get accomplished each day that we forget why we are doing it in the first place. We make ourselves so busy. We believe we are so vital to the operation of our work and business. We make ourselves out to be so important and significant as if somehow it's all going to collapse if we are not handling every little detail. We ignore those in our presence as we punch and prod our way through electric devices.

And then we get "farewell orders." We get another job. We move on. Funny. We look back and see that the place is still humming along without our involvement. A health concern arises. A marriage falls apart. A rebellious teenager sets a family into a tailspin. Didn't see that coming.

I am writing here out of the core of my soul to say I have been there. It's not a good space. It's when my ego is centered on my so-called "eternal throne." I engaged in this subject of rest because of needs in my own life and in what I observed in the lives of those I worked with. I experienced first-hand what its lack in my life can bring. I began to read my own press clippings, began to believe them, and somehow I walked around the planet thinking, "What a great gift of God I am to everyone. How will this place survive without me?" Hogwash. Pure hogwash.

I was letting the life I was supposed to be living slide by me without my honest engagement. I was drowning. Depressed. Discouraged. Add your "d" word here and I experienced it.

Then I stumbled upon this: "The apostles returned to Jesus from their ministry tour and told him all they had done and taught. Then Jesus said, "Let's go off by ourselves to a quiet place and rest awhile." He said this because there were so many people coming and going that Jesus and his apostles didn't even have time to eat."[15]

"Permission to rest, my Lord?"

"Tim. Tim. Tim. No permission needed, my love. My gift to you. Go play."

Pause.

"You sure, Jesus?"

Slow nod of the head.

"Mmhmm. Go."

"Oh, and Tim?"

"Yes, Jesus?"

"Make sure you eat. Remember to laugh. And. Laugh. You are good at making others happy."

There are verses of scripture that at times seemingly pop out at me while I am at certain stages in my life's journey. When it was all crashing down for me, this verse became one of a few others that kept me afloat.

Literally. I went away. Physically. To a desolate place. For two months. Where? London. Now don't get in a huff. London is far from desolate. It's one of my favorite places to visit in the world. I love the history. The culture, the people, and the accents are just lovely. The abundance of theater on the West End does the heart of this actor good. The culture. The people. The accents. The sights and sounds and smells. The food? Eh. Not so much. Picture a horizontal wavy hand here.

I had the privilege to come away with about twenty-five other colleagues from around the world to retreat with and be revived at something we call The Salvation Army International College for Officers. ICO. If you are into initials. Truly a God send.

At that time, I was away from my family and the demanding duties of my job for an extended period. My wife and I had the very distinct privilege of getting the first Ray & Joan Kroc Corps Community Center off the ground.[16] We were pioneers of sorts helping to guide The Salvation Army down this path to create and operate the first center of its kind. It was a huge undertaking that was full of blessings and burdens. While we were in the middle of getting this center up and going in San Diego, I was sent overseas for eight weeks to ICO.

I was able to spend time in silence, prayer, study, and in reflection. In prayer and reflection. In study. In discussion with others. I got to explore the beautiful country of the United Kingdom. I gained a deeper appreciation for the heritage of my denomination. I delved into my head and heart and was allowed permission to open up the rusting locks that barricaded my heart and allowed God full entry.

I learned the truth of what it meant to really let God have my burdens. I learned to live "lightly and freely" again. I learned not to take myself so seriously. Because no one else does. The pause allowed me to get back on track and in tune with the essentials: family, faith, fellowship, and fun. I haven't been the same since.

As you are reading this, perhaps you are in the same head space I was in then. I want to encourage you that you can truly navigate your way out of it. It may take some time. You may have to physically put yourself in a place where you can just think and release the burdens. You may have some good friends who really want to travel with you and help you along the unknown destination God is leading you. Maybe you just need to take more naps. Put the phone away for a day or two or even just for a meal.

You may need to just relax and focus awhile on certain scriptures. Like I did. Mark 6 is a great place to start.

I didn't do this recreating alone. God brought important people to me that held me accountable, helped me to experience joy again, and freely spoke truth into me when I didn't need to hear any more lies. This life goes quickly. Yeah. Yeah. Yeah.

No. Seriously it does. Listen to Emily again: "It goes so fast. We don't have time to look at one another."

How true that is even to this day.

We get one crack at this. Go out and have fun. Experience the true joy that comes when you enter in recreating yourself.

Just one favor please? No serious board games with me. It's all I ask. I will be over in the corner, searching for an easy board game to play, playing Candyland of course.

Questions for reflection
What is it you are doing these days to recreate yourself?

What does God's word say to you about play?

Are there self-imposed burdens that you need to let go of and let others carry for you?

Chapter
FIVE

~ *Delight* ~
Defining joy in our lives

"The true delight is in the finding out rather than in the knowing." ~ Isaac Asimov

"What truly makes you happy, Tim?" The question for the ages. Before I answer that, you need to know a few things about me. First, I am a natural born cynic. I am skeptical. Maybe it comes as a bonus with the gift of spiritual intuition that I have. It's called discernment. I can hardly take things at face value.

Slapstick humor never did it for me. I never understood the old TV show *The Three Stooges*. It's basically about three guys who get into trouble time and time again, and then they would always beat each other up. Moe was a bully and was always slugging everyone in the group. Larry was always getting his hair yanked out. He had the same hair part as me, so I felt sympathy. Curly wasn't curly. He was obese and obnoxious. He made weird noises and waved his hands. The humor of that show sailed way over my head.

Simple, mindless plots of cookie-cutter television comedy shows bore me. Insults and put-down humor just make me sad and angry. I have been around people who mask their insecurities by making fun of others. Not sure why my baldness needs to be the brunt of someone's joke, but I always seemed to be fair game. But whatever.

The "so what" question has to be answered. Just ask my former students. When I was teaching and serving for nine years at The Salvation Army College for Officer Training in Rancho Palos Verdes, CA, "So what, preacher, so what?" is a sound bite I would use to wrap up any sermon I was preaching. That phrase will be inscribed on my tombstone. Well. My imaginary one. The green trail at Camp Redwood Glen in the redwoods outside of Santa Cruz, CA, for me please, as my final resting spot. Word to my loved ones: ashes to ashes, dust to dust.

I like logistics. I need to know how things work. Take airplanes for instance. I like to know how it is we get a heavy piece of metal filled with human beings and flammable fuel some 35,000 feet up in the air. And back down again. Safely. Every day. All over the world.

Whenever I make a trip on an airplane that has a television screen in front of me, I set it to the world map. I like to know where we are. How far have we come on the trip? How long till we get there? And in case I decide to do some wing walking, what is the temperature outside? Usually minus subzero kabillion. I want to dress properly for it. How is that package I order online getting from point A to point B so quickly? Or not at all.

I used to ponder how a piece of paper I put in one end of a fax machine came out of another. How warming up my turkey hot dog in the microwave for forty seconds works. And who makes turkey hot dogs anyway, and how did they come up with that idea? How did we exactly get that man on the moon?

Things make me happy. But some things don't. Like. A poorly written and produced TV show or movie. Stop wasting my time and space. Bullies. Grumpy people. Unkind people. Bigoted people. Closed minded people. That's about 50% of us? Not sure, but close. Ice cream that makes me fat. Potato chips that are baked with some sort of chemicals that make my stomach flip more than a traveling flea circus. Overtly religious people who don't back up their talk with a godly walk. Exercise.

What? Hold on fella.

Look. I do it. But it doesn't make me happy. I don't worship my body. Recently I was told the "D" word would soon descend upon my body. "Get a gym membership. Oh. Drop the sugar and every carb known to humankind. Enjoy that celery, Mr. Foley," says my doctor with her sadistic smile. I lost twenty pounds. My "one pack" stomach has moved slowly to a "two pack." I have my exercise regimen now. But it doesn't make me happy. Back to that happy thought. That's easy peasy. I like to make others happy. I like to see joy come across the face of others. I like to lighten the moment with an instant dose of my lousy wit. To offer terrific improvisation in the moment. To see that soft ball lifted in an imaginary way above the board table and strike at it to stifle the moans and open the way for giggles. If my wife is sitting next to me in those moments, she touches my leg and softly says, "No."

But I can never resist. All the world is my stage. There is a captive audience here. Entertain. Make 'em happy.

I like to laugh with people who like to laugh. I like to be around people who are not pretentious (that is my word of the decade, by the way.) Who don't take themselves so seriously. Who know that life is much more than a position obtained or a title held or a piece of paper on the wall. Real, earthy, authentic people who want nothing from me but my presence.

Recently I was transformed by a book written by Amy Hollingsworth. *The Simple Faith of Mr. Rogers*. Truly a wonderful read. While reading the book, I was reminded of special people I will never forget. I have had a few of those along my journey so far, but certainly there is one encounter I will forever treasure. It was the day my wife and I met Mr. Fred Rogers and his wife, Joann, and gave them a personal tour of the first Salvation Army Ray & Joan Kroc Corps Community Center in San Diego in our capacity of administrators of the facility. He was a very dear friend of Joan Kroc. She had invited him to speak at the public dedication of this beautiful, state-of-the-art community center that she so generously supported and funded.

As we worked our way through the campus, I will never forget how engaged and kind Fred Rogers was to us. Asking us all sorts of questions, stopping to gaze at the facility often, he said, "Oh my, now isn't this just wonderful" so many times.

At the end of the tour, he stopped to thank Cindy and myself. He said, "This is quite a load and responsibility for you both. I don't know how you are going to do it. But I will pray for you." To be prayed for by Mr. Fred Rogers was indeed one of the biggest blessings I have ever had. I believe his prayers are one of the reasons we succeeded and have twenty-six Kroc Centers across our nation today.

Pioneering work was far from easy. But to have what I consider a divine engagement with one of the godliest and kindest men we have ever seen on the planet was worth all the heartache we went through.

The privilege to serve is mine. To serve suffering humanity. Wherever. Whenever. The life of service and surrender comes with no promises. No perks. No entitlements. No bonuses or fancy cars or private jet airplanes.

No warm and fuzzy feelings. No roar of the crowd. Just the smell of the grease trap in that kitchen where you help to make meals day in and day out for people who otherwise would go hungry. In the background. Out of the limelight. Out of sight. Certainly, out of people's minds.

That's what surrender looks like. No concern how of this will affect my "career path" or obsessing over where I will be tomorrow or at a certain time in my life.

Optics? How this looks? Who cares? None of that matters. When we pause, we can find delight in doing the things that make us happy. That is how God first intended it to be. But Adam and Eve got things mixed up and decided on a better way, which turned out to be way off the path God intended.

God gave us a commandant that says to stop. One day a week. Look around. Pause. Take it all in. It's all good. Then we messed it up. The earliest followers had to dig deeper into the weeds and add all sorts of amendments to the policy book.

You can't do this. Or that. Or even think that. Don't push that button. Don't pull your mule out of the ditch. (A daily problem for any of you?) Oh, if you do any of these things, we have to take you outside the city limits and stone you to death.

Delight

"You must keep the Sabbath day, for it is a holy day for you. Anyone who desecrates it must be put to death; anyone who works on that day will be cut off from the community."[17]

They took what was to be a delight and benefit to our sense of total well-being and turned it into a legalistic, mumble jumble that some still fret and fight over to this day. Over 600 something rules of "no" and "don't" supplanted the simple list of do: finding delight.

I have heard the following a few times in the past few years:

Them: "When are you going get that book done on that rest thing?"

Me: "Dunno. Soon. I hope."

Them: "Well I hope soon. I am looking for that explanation I can give to my boss backing up my stance of working only four days a week, for four hours a day, with forty days paid vacation."

Me: Blank stare.

Them: "Ha, ha."

Me: Watch them walk away.

This topic of sabbath rest isn't about a legalistic approach or anything anyone is entitled to. This is simply about learning how to embrace the commands of God and work them in such a way that they can bring us delight. We still judge ourselves harshly today, even though we do not take advice about sabbath seriously.

It's not a day of drudge. It's a day of delight. If that takes place on a Saturday, for every Saturday for the rest of your life, good on you. Just don't legislate that manner to others. Jesus spoke up against that. The religious people even ruined the day of rest.

If you are like me and grab it on the go, find those "sunbeam moments of rest" where you hit the pause button, intentionally slow down, listen to your body, and look into the eyes of those around you, all the better.

As I explained in the introduction, the phrase "beware of the machinery" has helped me navigate through life. The riddle that the Divisional Commander shared with me has been revealed in so many different ways I could fill page after page on stories I have experienced. I have been way too close to the machines, with loose clothing to boot that sucked me in and spit me out like a shredded piece of cloth. The machinery might consist of well-intentioned people. It could be all those "smart goals" you set for yourself. The lure of the career path and stepping over whomever to make your way down it could be part of the machine as well. It can be holy ambition masked in workaholism.

Maybe your view of who God really is needs to be rebooted. He takes no pleasure in our demise. As a father of three adult children, I can tell you I never took any great joy or pleasure in their disobedience. That never made me happy. What eventually brought me joy is how the lessons they learned in their individual failings shed light on their path and helped them never make those same mistakes again.

So what, preacher?

Shrugs. It's simple really. Find what makes you happy. Whatever is moral, legal, energizing, and draws you more into the presence of God. Stop over-thinking it. Put an end to manifesting a legal interpretation to it all.

Just do it. Be happy. Learn to be content. Stop running. Shut the spigot off to overwork and overindulgence, or undue diligence or self-incrimination. Seek to be centered again in the simple truths of God's word.

You can hear God say, "I made this day of rest. For you. Yes. You. Now, delight in it."

Questions for reflection

Make a list of what makes you happy. What are you doing to engage in it?

What parts of the machinery are starting to chew away at you?

Find sometime today to just laugh alone and with others. Note the experience.

Chapter SIX

~ *Celebration* ~
Delight in the life we have been given

"We think there is endless time to live but we never know which moment is last. So, share, care, love and celebrate every moment of life." ~ Anonymous

    The rules for birthday parties have changed since I was a kid. Back then you would simply show up to a party with a present, settle in, and enjoy treats such as cake and Kool-Aid, play some fun games like pin the tail on the donkey, and call it a day. Now if you throw a party, the expectation is that you have to rent a circus to come to your house and you must give favors to your guests before they leave. Who started this tradition?

    Birthdays are a special time to get together to celebrate. Some want the whole world to stop along with them to celebrate the fact that they exist. Some mourn over their birthday. Another year older, another day closer to death. Some are ambivalent towards it. For me, I choose to celebrate on the 0s and 5s. I don't like parties, and I don't like calling attention to my age, but I will share when asked.

    When my then three-year-old grandson, Callum, began to drill each of us around the table to tell him how old we were, I proudly told him, "I stretch, I kick, and I stretch again, because I am sixty, sixty years old!" He laughed out loud while the others just groaned and rolled their eyes. He asked me again and then told me to stop. Then he said, "Grandpa, you stretch, you kick, and you stretch again because you are sixty, sixty years old." The kid gets it. When we celebrate something, we are really pausing. We are taking a moment in time to stop, reflect, and rejoice. Whether it's as simple as a birthday or as complex as a retirement, taking the time to slow and have fun either by ourselves or with others is vital. Sabbath grants us a time of joy and celebration. We take the time to be reminded of the consistency of God's character and his faithfulness in our lives. When we practice sabbath we are able to focus on the truth of the matter that God is consistent in both his love and discipline in our lives. Even in the dark moments of individual and corporate suffering.

Marva Dawn writes, "It's not like our birthdays, which we celebrate because they happen only once a year. Rather, we celebrate every seven days because God's grace happens always."[18] God continues to choose to love his creatures and creation within the time and space he has created. His love and grace never give up on any of us. That thought alone should stop us in our tracks to give thanks and find joy.

Dan Allendar refers to sabbath in a unique way. He writes, "The sabbath is our play day—not as a break from the routine of work, but as a feast that celebrates the superabundance of God's creative love, to give glory for no other reason other than love himself, love to create and give away glory."[19]

We can intentionally pick a time to stop and celebrate all that has been given to us. God created everything and he found it was good. He intended for his creation to stop and rest, to find great joy and satisfaction in labor, and to find restoration for the work that lies ahead.

Celebration can swiftly turn into the accumulation of things, the need to do and prepare instead of simply appreciating how things are. We can too easily neglect to notice God in the simple things of life and in the silence. Marva Dawn frankly states, "Our society has forgotten how to celebrate. It has associated celebration with dissipation. It has turned the festival of the birth of Christ into a gluttonous spending spree and the festival of the resurrection of Christ into a spring egg roll and candy hunt."[20]

Celebration

We groan when credit card bills arrive in our mail mid-January. We frown when we step on the scale and see how much we have gained after consuming too much Easter candy.

Taking time to celebrate is not selfish in nature. We are not to retreat into some sort of cave or bubble and forget the world in need around us. Resting in the grace of God reminds us that we can joyfully embrace and relish the work we face and the events of life that come our way.

We are given many opportunities to serve others and are blessed by doing. So, by joyfully embracing my rest, I am rejuvenated to continue to reach out to others. Stopping for rest gives me more energy, renews my vision, and expands my horizons as I see clearly the challenges that await and how to best handle them.

Questions for reflection
What do you celebrate in your life?

What sort of celebrations energize or drain you?

Do you see how pausing at least once a week can benefit you? How so?

Chapter SEVEN

~ *Ceasing* ~
Hitting the stop button

"When I cease to enjoy what I'm doing, then I shall do something mundane—like clean my house."
~ Peggy Toney Horton

    The term "ceasing" is a foreign concept to me. It has certainly been the opposite of how I have viewed myself over nearly four decades of ministry. If truth be told, I hardly know what the definition is without having to look it up.
    Even on the days where I have scheduled a disengagement of sorts, the tyranny of the urgent looms over my mind. Often it invades my sleep. I dream of conversations with people I know. Work matters rise up in my imagination when I am sitting still. A mental to-do list grows rapidly as I dwell on all that needs to be done. The challenge for getting that list cleared outweighs just letting the list sit and ferment.
    Marva Dawn comments on the idea of ceasing: "The more we think about resting, the more we realize that we have to set many things aside to engage in it. We can't truly rest if our minds are going at supersonic speed. We can't genuinely savor a sabbath day if we insist on 'accomplishing' things, even if what we do is for God."[21]
    One of the most profound thoughts I stumbled across in all of my studies on this subject is from author Howard Baker: "Primarily, I have lost my soul to one of the chief rivals of devotion to Christ—that is, service for Him."[22] How ironic that even

my own devotion to service in the Kingdom of God can lead to my own downfall by preventing me from engaging in refusing the discipline of ceasing.

Sabbath is simply all about stopping. Desist. It's the forgoing of the need to forge on ahead and complete the long to-do list that I carry around in my hand (also known as my smart phone).

Thomas Merton writes, "There are times, then, when in order to keep ourselves in existence at all we simply have to sit back for a while and do nothing. And for a man who has let himself be drawn completely out of himself by his activity, nothing is more difficult than to sit still and rest, doing nothing at all. The very act of resting is the hardest and most courageous act he can ever perform: and it is quite beyond his power."[23]

Changing the title of my to-do list to a "to-be-done-later list" is a step in the right direction. Giving myself permission to stop is vital. I work in a ministry where stopping has not been cultivated or talked about over the years. Most of us, if we were completely honest with ourselves, do not stop. We often don't know how to stop. We either do not choose to or we do not know how to cease. Or we think that somehow we are so significant to the operation of our little worlds that if we simply stop for one moment, the axis will tilt, and all will be lost.

A dynamic for any athlete is that they must learn to listen to their body. One cannot work out seven days a week without eventually encountering some serious wear and tear. The sting of pain is a warning sign that the body is trying to say stop. A devoted runner must cease from all training and competition from time to time in order to be fit, rested, and restored for the next race. The simple reality is this: there is never, nor will there ever be, enough time to get everything done. The sooner one comprehends this, the better off one will be in the long run. But the fact of the matter is we do not let our pursuit go. Learning to cease is a challenge for the 21st century warrior.

Donna Schaper writes, "Sabbath is the separation of work from play, leisure from obligation, and duty from grace. It used to be a day, now it's a pattern. Sabbath is being off in a world where the eleventh commandment is to be on."[24] She hits the nail on the head here with the comment of the unwritten 11th commandment, which has become the new normal in most first world settings. Even while one is on vacation, the need to be plugged in is great.

What is it we are ceasing from exactly? The sabbath calls us to stop working. "Remember to observe the Sabbath day by keeping it holy. You have six days each week for your ordinary work, but the seventh day is a Sabbath day of rest dedicated to the Lord your God. On that day no one in your household may do any work. This includes you, your sons and daughters, your male and female servants, your livestock and any foreigners living among you."[25]

Defining what constitutes work has to come into play here. What some may consider to be an abomination on the sabbath day, like fiddling with your cell phone or computer, might be something of pure joy to another.

For some, ceasing may involve taking a long walk in the forest or slipping into a deep, sound slumber on a cold afternoon. For others it may involve taking in a movie, building furniture, going to local museums, or enjoying a warm beverage with friends at the local coffee shop. I enjoy getting lost in one of my favorite video games or spending time with my model trains and their make-believe land. Anything that takes you away from the daily grind can truly work and bring you closer to God in the process.

Anything you can do that brings you delight, helps you to be calm, and centers you so as to equip you for the work ahead is a good thing. Mark Buchanan writes, "Most of the things we need to be most fully alive never come in busyness. They grow in rest."

Allow ceasing to be a part of your weekly routine. You are the only one who can make that happen.

Questions for reflection

When you hear the term "cease," what immediately runs through your mind?

Make a list of things you long to cease from.

How can you make ceasing a part of your weekly routine?

Chapter EIGHT

~ *Sabbath* ~
We rest to work

"Even if people fail to observe the Sabbath, it remains holy."
~ Abraham Herschel

    To be honest, I have been dragging my heels to write and produce this book. Not because there isn't any interest, nor because I don't know how to write. Heaven knows I have studied, read, discussed, taught, and wrote on the subject more than anything else in the past five years of my life. I have become known as "that Sabbath guy." But one of my reasons for reluctance is that some may view this as an end all to what true rest in God means. I am still in the process of discovering it myself.
    This isn't a book about justifying a simple work week. People have to work to survive. Many people in our day and age have to work numerous jobs just to pay the rent or mortgage and to keep their heads above water. Many in the millennial generation are drowning in student loans and personal debt, still living at home, never seeing the end in sight. That has become the unfortunate norm.
    Over the years it has been my extreme privilege to be invited to teach in several developing countries. This has often been one of the most beneficial and eye-opening experiences I have ever encountered. Getting out of my stereotypical North American mindset and entering into a foreign land, with its different customs, challenges, and daily rhythms, is truly invigorating.
    In one of the countries where I recently taught, one Salvation

Army leader told me that the officers in his territory do not know what rest means. It was breaking his heart. Some officers were literally dying because of exhaustion. They were not eating right and had no sense of balance in their lives. There was no play. Little sleep. The spirit of joy has evaporated from their souls.

These people often work in very harsh and rugged areas seven days a week. In one place I visited, it was customary for the officers to be up at 3 a.m. to begin prepping for the meals that they would be cooking for the people under their care that coming day. They rarely take a vacation. Never exploring any "me time" options. They are devoted to caring for their people and proclaiming God's word.

I know good works don't get us into heaven, but I think these people will probably have a closer view of the throne than I will. Their selfless devotion puts me to shame.

In my teaching, I simply pleaded with them to stop. They were not asking for a two-day-off option. They were struggling to even make themselves come to the point of realizing that they were really in violation of what God wanted from them. And that is to stop.

For we rest to work. Not work to rest. We often have that backwards. God created us to sleep to allow our bodies to recreate themselves for the day of work that comes with the rising sun.

The Jews celebrate the Sabbath from sundown to sundown on Friday and Saturday. Christians partake in Sabbath on Sunday as a celebration of the resurrection of Jesus. But as a Salvation Army officer, Sunday, for me, has been the most hectic and busiest day of the week. It is not the ideal day for me or my colleagues to set aside and cease from my activities. We have a job to do. We have a congregation to lead, outreach to perform, Sunday services to supervise. So, I search for other times in my week where I can have the divine appointment of delighting in ceasing and resting.

Over the course of my study on this subject, I have encountered some individuals who approach the Sabbath legalistically. One responder in the research project I was working on wrote, "I separated from The Salvation Army because they do not recognize 7th Day, nor His Name, nor His appointed times." Ouch.

That was a pretty harsh comment in my eyes. I often wonder what all the steps this individual took to come up with that conclusion. There is always context to our stories. Opinions are derived from experiences. A legalistic interpretation of what day to take is common, but to say The Salvation Army doesn't recognize his name is something else.

The most profound and frank comment I read on what sabbath is not came from Dan Allender: "Many who take the sabbath seriously and intentionally ruin it with legislation and worrisome fences that protect the sabbath but destroy its delight. For many sabbath keepers, it is a day of duty, diligence and spiritual focus that eschews play and pleasure for Bible reading, prayer, naps and tedious religious services that seem designed to suck the air out of the soul. If that is keeping the sabbath holy, then it's better to break it."[26]

Another person asked me directly in the survey, "How do you expect to change the Army's culture?" My simple response is I don't expect to change it. That is not my goal. To stand in the streets in front of International Headquarters with a burning torch demanding change was never something I envisioned. To cause some sort of "revolution on rest" is not the aim here. Getting an individual to think about creating intentional space in their lives is at the heart of what I propose.

Getting back to the machinery metaphor for a moment, changing processes for the overall organizational structure takes place slowly and does eventually happen when push comes to shove. The Salvation Army is made up of individuals filled with the power of God through his Holy Spirit. The change I argue for is individual, not institutional. I can only look to God's word for myself and feed my soul on the impressions given to me. I can't depend on other people to make the changes to my life that I know I need to make. If I choose to burn the candle at both ends and see myself going down in flames as some sort of martyr, well, that is on me. I personally don't believe that is what God is calling any of us to do.

On one hand, because we in The Salvation Army do not abide

by some strict interpretation of sabbath, there are individuals who would rather not be a part of this serving community and will try to find some place that will view sabbath as they do. On the other hand, the never ending and relentless call for those serving in The Salvation Army to do more is foundational. It's in our DNA: "that and better will do," were mission words from the founder, William Booth. The internal culture is so ingrained in doing the most good, taking a break from that can be seen by some as lazy, unnecessary, or a waste of time.

To be fair, I don't expect this book to be the agent to resolve the endless debates on the matter. I can hear the push back already. I also didn't set out to change the way an individual views sabbath within the context of the organization, denomination, or personal preference. In a chapter of my dissertation,[27] I mentioned the generous offering of time off that the average officer is given. And yet half of the active officer force I surveyed (in the Western Territory) do not even make use of time allowed to be away from their heavy ministry responsibilities. That became a personal issue for me. I have seen the breakdowns in health and marriage relationships due to the addiction to work. Burning the candle at both ends usually means the candle comes to an end. Eventually both wick and wax disappear.

It's not necessary. God really doesn't need any heroes. He needs rested and equipped warriors who wage the war of love in a hostile world.

In response to one of my sample questions, a responder stated the following challenge: "The Salvation Army is a ministry and ministry is busy...We are to be about OTHERS, but many times we are worn out from taking care of OTHERS and we can't give what we don't have."

That begs the question: whose fault is that? Is it a system or is it me letting the system rule the process of rest in my life?

The need to develop sabbath as a spiritual discipline exists within the work force of my colleagues and in the context of my own journey. The work will never end. If my friends and I do not seek to cease, rest, and embrace sabbath, we will not be able to carry on the work of helping others. This can be said of anyone engaged in full-time ministry or anyone on the face of the earth. We must pause and rest. That is what we were created for.

While on this study, I was drawn to several passages of scripture in both testaments. The command of keeping the sabbath arises from the Old Testament: "Remember the Sabbath day by keeping it holy. Six days you shall labor and do all your work, but the seventh day is a sabbath to the Lord your God. On it you shall not do any work, neither you, nor your son or daughter, nor your male or female servant, nor your animals, nor any foreigner residing in your towns. For in six days the Lord made the heavens and the earth, the sea, and all that is in them, but he rested on the seventh day. Therefore, the Lord blessed the sabbath day and made it holy."[28]

God set the Sabbath day for the Israelites to spend unhurried time in worship and rest. God's initial concern for his creation to rest was there in the beginning: "So, the creation of the heavens and the earth and everything in them was completed. On the seventh day God had finished his work of creation, so he rested from all his work. And God blessed the seventh day and declared it holy, because it was the day when he rested from all his work of creation."[29]

Rest is to be entered willfully and intentionally into. In the midst of all my busyness in kingdom work, if I fail to take time to rest and worship, I obviously do not think much of God's place in my life.

This command is not an ancient directive without a premise or a purpose. There is a great benefit that comes to me when I adhere to it. He tells us to slow down, stop, cease from all that entangles us, and embrace this day. Sabbath is not a day where I focus on what I don't do, but rather it's a time when I can truly designate to be in God's presence, both now and in the week to come.

The prophet Isaiah conveys God's intention precisely: "If you keep your feet from breaking the sabbath and from doing as you please on my holy day, if you call the sabbath a delight and the Lord's holy day honorable, and if you honor it by not going your own way and not doing as you please or speaking idle words, then you will find your joy in the Lord, and I will cause you to ride in triumph on the heights of the land and to feast on the inheritance of your father Jacob. For the mouth of the Lord has spoken."[30]

This passage reminds me that I do not always know what is best for me. Sabbath rest is an honorable event to participate in some fashion, weekly. God promises that when I embrace and engage in it, joy and delight are mine. The everyday events of my life can sometimes be overwhelming. When I take this time to singularly focus on rest, things change. I begin to see that God is truly bigger than any problem I might be facing. God desires greatly to be a part of the solution. Honoring sabbath rest individually and in community replenishes my reservoirs and allows me to immerse myself in the needs of others.

Questions for reflection
Do you regularly practice sabbath? Why or why not?

How does your life reflect this biblical mandate?

Do a survey of your week. Keep track of what you do every hour for a solid week.

Is there adequate time for rest?

Chapter NINE

~ *A Day Off* ~
The call to something different

*"Sometimes I just wish I had a day off.
I really need to clean my room."*
~ Lizzy McGuire

    In all the years I have been engaged in ministry work, only in one appointment was it clear from the get-go that a regular day off was pretty much set in stone on the calendar. When we arrived on the beautiful island of Maui, HI, one of the first things emphasized to me was that all of the "Kahunas" (spiritual leaders) on the island took Mondays off as their sabbath time. No argument about this from me. I embraced it.

    How that proved to be important for Cindy and me. It worked for us, personally and for our marriage. We were given permission to stop. To lay the work to the side and just find ways to be refreshed. We were living in paradise, after all, so why not enjoy it? I haven't had that experience since.

    One of the biggest takeaways that I have gained over the years from personal reflection and the discipline of academic study on sabbath is what it is not.

    Sabbath is not a day off. It's not a day that I simply just stop doing one task and replace it with another long litany of undertakings to complete. It is a holy day. It is a day in which I must separate myself completely, disengaging from my busyness so I may attend to the business of soul care.

Sabbath rest is different from an ordinary day off. The norm of a typical week for an individual engaged in pastoral ministry varies and shifts depending on situations, crises, and other pressing matters that arise. Pastors often struggle with the challenge of attempting to take time away for reflection and rest when the norm never formalizes. Fear of losing face or the pressure of being a part of a culture that requires one to be on 24/7 can literally consume the heart of a pastor.

In her article entitled, "Sabbath for Clergy," Donna Schaper advocates for the need for clergy to take two days off a week. She writes, "Clergy may never have a predictable and regular period of time off, but they always need to have two full days off. The days may come as soccer on Thursday and opera on Tuesday. But they still need a total of two days or four units (a unit being a morning or an afternoon). Otherwise our work will suffer, and we will burn out."[31]

She goes on to stress some very practical reasons why this should be the case: "Because we need two days off, one for the laundry and one for sabbath. On a regular basis we should work mornings and nights or afternoons and nights, never both, and never both six or seven days in a row."[32]

To free the mind of the clergy member from any irrational guilt, she continues: "Remember the norm. Remember what other people work. Imagine your humanity and work like you are 'other' people, not more and not less."

The practical reality I have encountered in the seasons of my journey in full-time ministry is that many settings I found myself in prevented this from happening. Schaper offers some food for thought here and it should be considered. But is it practical and obtainable? Although this may be the ideal that can work in one ministry setting, other people who read this might feel guilty because the demands of their current circumstances prevent them from doing so. Again, finding balance, as cliché as it might sound, needs to be struck.

For instance, outside of taking furlough (vacation), I have never been able to find a way to habitually put two days off together

A Day Off

to take off in over thirty-eight years of full-time ministry. Does that mean I am at odds with the command of God? No. It simply means that I am not able to reach this ideal. I am envious of those who can. But my focus is on what I can do, when I can do it, and to make sure I engage in a deep, meaningful sabbath in the process.

All work and no time for play can lead to an innumerable amount of complications and physical and mental health issues including anxiety and depression. Facing the fact that there are always crises to attend to, paperwork to shovel, and obligations to fulfill can lead us into what Schaper calls becoming a "human doing" instead of a human being. In order for you to get your life in order, you need to work ahead and revel in the reality of flextime. She writes, "Accept that you are swimming upstream. Understand that the true keeping of sabbath is an act of non-violent disobedience. Expect punishments. Expect suspicion. Expect and anticipate the guilt trip of 'she is not working as hard as I am.' Be ready to have a good laugh next time someone tells you that you only work on Saturday or Sunday."[33]

Often times the biggest obstacle that lies in the way of grasping on to the concept of ceasing is ourselves. I have struggled with the fact that when I relax, I may feel as if I am wasting time, that there are things I should be attending to.

Lynne Baab writes, "Do you work for pay? If so, then stopping any job activities on your sabbath is a good place to start." If you type a lot, don't type. If you use a lot of technology in your work, then avoid the computer on your sabbath. Make a lot of phone calls in your typical week? No calls. Driving a lot of miles in your job? Let the car remain parked. In other words, let the reminders of work be tabled."

Pausing to reflect and rest and finding a place for solace and silence in these times allows us to release the worries we lug around. We can truly learn to "cast our cares on Him." But there is a danger when we create this sort of space in our lives. Negative thinking can creep in. Dorothy Bass retells the story of Abraham Heschel writing about a pious man who was walking around his vineyard on a Sabbath. He saw a broken fence and thought he would come back the next day to fix it. When he realized he thought of this act on the Sabbath, he thought to himself that it was wrong to think that and that he should never repair it. His extreme reasoning came from interpreting the ancient Sabbath commandment: rest even from the thought of labor.

In pointing out how such a commandment is nearly impossible to obey, Bass offers a better take: "We can refrain from activities that we know will summon worry, activities like paying bills, doing tax returns, and making lists of things to do in the coming week... we can cultivate those forms of engagement with nature, ideas and other people that really get our mind off the week ahead."[34]

Sabbath rest goes much deeper than just sitting down and doing nothing or ceasing to zoom around town on errands or even taking that much needed nap. That plays into it, but that's not it. The obstacles to creating space for sabbath rest are subtle. We can easily attempt to settle on tomorrow as the day of rest and ignore making the most of the todays that come to us as sabbath.

Alan Falding writes, "Unfortunately, when it comes to rest, we tend to turn 'today' into 'someday.' Someday, I'll live a more restful life. When I get out of college and start my career...When I get married and start a family...when I get established in my life and my job...When I retire...When I die? When will we 'enter God's rest?' We default to that out of reach 'someday' whenever we offer up our 'not yet' excuses. Sometimes it's a seasonal 'yet': I just can't afford the time right now; or an emotional 'not yet': No one else is doing it."[35]

The illusive tomorrow is here in the present. It will pay off dividends if one will stop, rest, and reflect. The outcome of you can be easily recharged and re-energized for the work that lies ahead.

Questions for reflection
Have I been able to truly take the time to rest?

If I am not entering this gift of rest, what is preventing me from doing so?

Chapter
TEN

~ *So what?* ~
Further steps to take

"You can live as a ghost, waiting for death to come, or you can dance." ~ Alan Gratz

   That phrase "beware of the machinery" that I shared in this book was very wise counsel I received from a seasoned Salvation Army officer. They serve both as a warning and as a guide over the years of my active service as a Salvation Army officer. I hear the whirl of the machines in my daily grind. The particular machine I hear whispers out to me: "Do the most good." "Need has no season." "Heart to God. Hand to man." The sanctified slogans spew forth, all good, all solid, and all reasonable, motivational phrases for me to press on the upward way.

   What machine do you hear? What is it saying to you? If I plug away at this work with a pace that doesn't include rest and play, what is the expense I will have to pay? Will my relationships still be intact? Will my work have purpose and meaning? Am I trampling over others on my way to the top? Is my health declining more with each passing day simply because I don't know how to stop? Will my children have fond memories of my time with them, or was I preoccupied elsewhere?

   I have written this in the context of my life. What has been nearly four decades of active service as a Salvation Army officer has given me a world of opportunities that I have zero regret fulfilling. It has been a divine calling. It has been exhausting at times and exhilarating at other periods. A call that has compelled me and still urges me to share the gospel is, "with the least of these." I can't run from that. But that call doesn't mean I must ruin the essence of who I am mentally, emotionally, physically, and spiritually. Nor does it mean I must ruin the lives of others around me by my insistent need to be needed and to prove myself by my work. What happens to anyone that is just living in the "burning the candle at both ends" motif? If we continue on at a pace that doesn't allow for rest or see no real value in ceasing, what's the point? What happens to any of us when we ignore the fourth commandment of God?

The simple warning is that if we as individuals that make up an organization continue at these supersonic speeds and continue to ignore the need for sabbath, our ranks may dwindle. What's worse, spiritual atrophy will set in. Emotional and physical energy levels will begin to tank. Holy motivation will become lost in the fog of physical exhaustion.

The time, I believe, has come to not approach this subject with meekness or feign an ignorant understanding of its meaning. We must study it. We must teach and preach it. We must live it. We must not approach it as a trendy thing that only pertains to one generation. By all means we must not let it be a wedge used to divide us by any strict interpretation.

Let's be very clear: Sabbath is not a day off. It is not to be bathed in legalism in its approach. Rather, it is to be embraced and celebrated. It is not furlough time. It is not an extended time away from the duties at hand. These points I have attempted to hammer home here are the great take away from my in-depth study on the topic of sabbath rest.

Practicing sabbath rest is simply a vital means to gain our central rhythm back as we become more Christ-like in every way. We must truly learn how to cease from our work, rest in our Lord, celebrate our journey, and embrace the opportunities that sabbath affords us.

We learn the habits of intentionally creating space so that we can hear from God. So we can think. So we can recreate our

So what?

bodies and be recharged for the work that needs to be done.

I conclude with this in mind: I must at all cost avoid being swallowed up by the machinery of life. Whatever that may look like to you, understand that the machine will destroy you if you let it. You might get sucked into working so much that your life becomes a blur. Your soul becomes cold and calloused. You risk losing your purpose for living.

I must pay attention to the rhythms of my soul. I must notice and pay more heed to the movements of God in my life. I must make room to ponder and to pause, to play, to enjoy, and create more space and to embrace the delight of hearing the heartbeat of God. Sabbath rest can move out of the pages of theology and the halls of debate to become something I embrace and all the more so as I hear the machines humming.

Questions for reflection

What is your sabbath plan? Consider writing out your thoughts on the matter.

God is calling you to rest. What does that look like to you?

What are some significant takeaways from this book for you?

Epilogue

The final touches of this book were put together during the height of the COVID-19 pandemic that raced across the world like an out-of-control brush fire. The editorial team I work with had to do their jobs remotely for several weeks. Travel bans had been in place. Gatherings of ten or more people were banned. "Social distancing" was the norm and we were strongly encouraged to stay six feet away from each other. There was a great disconnect in places that we weren't used to.

In some parts of the world, even taking a simple walk was out of the question. It was against the law. Limited access to grocery stores and pharmacies was allowed, but in simple terms, most people felt like they were prisoners in their own homes. All in a massive attempt to curb this virus which had no cure at the time and left many people dead.

A "new normal" ruled the day. We worked from our homes. We were encouraged to keep a routine, reach out via technology to our friends, family, and work mates. And to make sure our neighbors were staying well.

The entire planet was in rest mode. Air traffic was cut in half. Air pollution dipped to all-time lows. Live sporting events, theater, and activities like going to the gym or even a barber shop stopped.

It wasn't readily embraced by all. Some thought they were immune from the virus because they didn't fit the age profile. Sadly, that was proven wrong. People of all ages got sick. A side effect from the stoppage is that many were going stir crazy after being cooped up for so long.

But many people did embrace the opportunity. It was a time stop. Albeit enforced by governments, businesses had no choice but to close; people were at home either by themselves or with loved ones. With schools closed, parents had to learn how to home school and be with their children all day long. Creative ways to play and to connect with others rose up. Physical rest began to rule the day. For the first time, many of us had nothing to do, nowhere to be, and no one to impress.

And it was a good thing.

Sabbath rest isn't something to be forced on any one nor should it be something rejected. In the period of the pandemic, new rhythms were adapted and put into place. Rest ruled our days.

Life eventually gets back to a pace that seems normal but can quickly become out of control or even unbearable. My hope is that rest will and can be a part of your everyday life. There is incredible value to slowing the pace and embracing the open spaces that become available to us. Working and resting go hand in hand. Rest adds to our physical and emotional well-being, but it also aids in helping us go deeper and learning to lean more into the ways of God and less into the ways of ourselves.

Rest is for you. Rest is a gift. Open it daily in your life.

Acknowledgments

I didn't write this in a vacuum. I didn't escape to some quiet space to write this all in one setting. Putting this together has been a process. From the first moments at Enders Island in Connecticut where God impressed on my heart that I must embrace sabbath in my life and to study and write about to the formation of these pages, I am a grateful man.

To my partner in ministry and marriage for the past thirty-five years, my wife, Cindy. Thank you for your unending love, support, tolerance, and constant encouragement through this process of studying sabbath rest. You are the smartest woman I know. Your intuition is amazing. Let's try to perfect this rest in the remaining thirty plus years we have together.

To my mentors and friends of both past and present: Dr. Stephen Macchia, who guided me through my doctorate program and taught me incredible things about my own spiritual formation. Dr. Fred Ross, long gone from this world who taught me to think for myself and continue to serve humanity with passion and Godly love. Lt. Colonel Rich Love, my former boss, who taught me the value of understanding that influence is truly greater than power. Commissioner Dave Hudson, who has been with me through thick and thin for over thirty years. I have learned more than I can say from these men of God.

To members of my D.Min. cohort, Dr. David Currie, and the support staff of Gordon-Conwell Theological Seminary Doctor of Ministry office. For being a part of my original journey on this important subject.

To my administrative assistants over the past several years: first while I was in the painful process of putting the dissertation project together, Celeste Skinner was a rock star. I would have never had it published in the first place without you. To

Kathleen Sperry and Kenya Hughes, who, in the past several years, have offered me protection and kept my calendar and my life in order. Thank you for bringing order in my life, keeping my professional path intact, and being brave enough to help me keep sacred space in my life.

To my predecessor, Lt. Colonel Allen Satterlee, who told me I had something here and I just need to pound it out in a narrative. Thank you for the encouragement. I finally did it.

To my editorial director, Jeff McDonald, and Major Jason Swain, for pouring over the content, striking my overuse of "but" and "it" and "and"; and for giving me encouraging feedback as this all came together.

Special thanks to Alexanderia Saurman, for careful editing and pulling this together for print. Joshua Morales, for your gift of visual effects with this book. Also special thanks to Ashley Schena and Elizabeth Hanley for last minute edits.

For the team at Versa Press in Peoria, IL. Your good work amazes me.

For the Salvation Army. The lifetime of ministry opportunity I have had is difficult to express.

To my fellow officers, soldiers, and friends of the Salvation Army, let's be brave enough to hit the stop button now and again in our lives.

To my mother, Rollys, who taught me the value of reading and who was proud of anything I did. I am sure she would have loved reading this. In like twenty minutes! She was a rapid reader. Mom, we will talk about it later in heaven together.

To my father, Gerry, who taught me never to quit or give up on anything. I hope you enjoy this book, dad. You gave us a wonderful childhood in which my siblings, Mike, Liz, Lyn, and Katy, along with myself, were able to play, laugh, love, and have fun.

Lastly, I thank God for my adult children, Laura, Alex, and Victoria, along with my grandson, Callum. You all continue to inspire me to play, to laugh, and to stick around long enough to see you all grow in this life to come.

Recommended Reading

My exploration on this subject will continue until my last breath. There is an incredibly long litany of books that have been written on this subject. The following is simply a sample of books you may want to consider for further study and reflection.

Allender, Dan B and Phyills Tickle. *Sabbath*. Nashville, TN: Thomas Nelson, 2009.

Buchanan, Mark. *The Rest of God: Restoring Your Soul by Restoring Sabbath*. Nashville, TN: W Pub. Group, 2006.

Calhoun, Adele Ahlberg. *Spiritual Disciplines Handbook: Practices That Transform Us*. Downers Grove, IL: InterVarsity Press, 2005.

Dawn, Marva J. *Keeping the Sabbath Wholly*. Grand Rapids, MI: William B. Eerdmans Publishing, 1989.

Fadling, Alan. *An Unhurried Life: Following Jesus' Rhythms of Work and Rest*. Downers Grove, IL: InterVarsity Press, 2013.

Hansel, Tim. *When I Relax I Feel Guilty*. Elgin, IL: D.C. Cook Pub., 1979.

Heschel, Abraham Joshua. *The Sabbath: Its Meaning For Modern Man*. New York: Farrar, Straus and Giroux, 2005.

Macchia, Stephen A. *Crafting a Rule of Life: An Invitation to the Well-ordered Way.* Downers Grove, IL: IVP Books, 2012.

Muller, Wayne. *Sabbath: Finding Rest, Renewal, and Delight in Our Busy Lives.* New York: Bantam Books, 2000.

Endnotes

1 Jeremiah 6:16
2 For further reading, see Exodus 20:1-21
3 Exodus 20:8
4 See Exodus 16
5 John 12:8
6 Mark 2:27-28
7 See Mark 6:1-3; Mark 2:23-27
8 Mark 2:23-27
9 1 Samuel 21:1-6
10 Fear Of Missing Out.
11 See I Corinthians 13
12 1 Corinthians 13:3b
13 1 Corinthians 13:5-7
14 http://www.whysanity.net/monos/town.html
15 Mark 6:30-31
16 See www.kroccenter.org for more information about this very unique ministry.
17 Exodus 31:14
18 Marva J. Dawn, *Keeping the Sabbath Wholly* (Grand Rapids, MI Eerdmans Publishing, 1989), 197.
19 Dan B. Allendar and Phyllis Tickle, *Sabbath* (Nashville, TN Thomas Nelson, 2009), 82.
20 Dawn, *Keeping the Sabbath Wholly*, 196
21 Marva J. Dawn, *The Sense of Call: A Sabbath way of Life for those who serve God, the church and the World*, (Grand Rapids, MI: W.B. Eerdmans Pub., 2006), 46
22 Howard Baker, *Soul Keeping: Ancient Paths of Spiritual Direction* (Colorado Springs, CO NavPress, 1998), 34
23 Thomas Merton, *No Man is an Island* (Boston MA. Shambhala, 2005), 123
24 Donna Schaper, *Sabbath for Clergy* (The Clergy Journal, May 2008), 12
25 Exodus 20:8-11
26 Allender and Tickle, *Sabbath*, 8.
27 Foley, Timothy, *Beware of the Machinery, The Sabbath & The Salvationist*. A doctoral thesis project on file at the library of Gordon-Conwell Theological Seminary, 2015
28 Exodus 20:8-11
29 Genesis 2:1-3
30 Isaiah 58:13-14
31 Schaper, *Sabbath for Clergy*, 12
32 Schaper, *Sabbath for Clergy*, 12
33 Schaper, *Sabbath for Clergy*, 12
34 Dorothy C. Bass, *Receiving the Day: Christian Practices for Opening the Gift of Time* (San Francisco, CA Jossey-Bass Publishers, 2000), 65.
35 Alan Falding, *An Unhurried Life, Following Jesus' Rhythms of Work and Rest* (Downers Grove, IL. InterVarsity Press, 2013), 122.

About the Author

Lt. Colonel Tim Foley has been a follower of Jesus Christ since 1978. In 1982, he was commissioned as a Salvation Army Officer. In 1985, he married Salvation Army Officer Cindy Hill. Together over the years, they have served in Oxnard, CA, Maui, HI, Phoenix and Mesa, AZ, San Diego, San Francisco, and Alexandria, VA.

They were the first administrators for The Salvation Army Ray and Joan Kroc Corps Community Center, in San Diego, responsible for the startup operations for this arts, education, and recreation center. Besides Corps Officer appointments, they have served as Divisional Youth Leaders, Training Leaders for the College for Officer Training in Rancho Palos Verdes, CA, and Divisional Leaders of the Golden State Division in California. He currently serves as National Secretary for Program and Editor-in-Chief at National Headquarters in Alexandria, VA.

Tim has a background in theatre and has been trained professionally as an actor and stage manager. He has been an advocate for the fine arts and education throughout his entire service with The Salvation Army. He holds a masters degree in theology (Fuller Theological Seminary) and a doctorate in spiritual formation for ministry leaders (Gordon Conwell Theological Seminary).

The Foleys have traveled and taught extensively in many places in the world. He enjoys writing and has written numerous articles for publication. In his spare time, he enjoys reading, participating in community theater, and collecting model trains. The Foley's have three adult children and one grandson.

For contact information for speaking and teaching engagements, email restforusall@gmail.com. Follow on Facebook @restforus.